HAL LEONARD
BASS METHOD

R&B BASS
BY GLENN LETSCH

To access audio visit:
www.halleonard.com/mylibrary

Enter Code
7040-5393-7497-9234

ISBN 978-0-634-07370-0

7777 W. BLUEMOUND RD. P.O. BOX 13819 MILWAUKEE, WI 53213

Copyright © 2005 by HAL LEONARD CORPORATION
International Copyright Secured   All Rights Reserved

For all works contained herein:
Unauthorized copying, arranging, adapting, recording, Internet posting, public performance, or other distribution of the printed or
recorded music in this publication is an infringement of copyright.
Infringers are liable under the law.

Visit Hal Leonard Online at
www.halleonard.com

CONTENTS

ACKNOWLEDGMENTS

Thanks to:

My wife Anne and my daughter Alysia

Uwe Salwender and Udo Klempt-Giessing of Glockenklang bass amplifiers

John Mader (drums and percussion)

Jeff Tamelier (guitars)

Rock Hendrix (sax)

Jerry Martin at Master Control Studio

Masaki Liu at One Way Studio

John Xepoleas

PREFACE

This book is intended to prepare the aspiring bassist for proficiency in the style of R&B. Classic songs are presented with accompanying audio. Scales, chords, etc. are included in a theoretical primer at the beginning of the book. Then we move on to these great songs. The sequence of songs progresses from easier to more difficult, generally speaking. This should keep your enthusiasm escalating as you accomplish the various techniques needed to master each classic track. The goal is not to just play these tunes down. The transcribed bass lines are exactly as heard on the original recordings, and the accompanying text should help you understand what's going on. Be sure to read the commentary for each tune. Hopefully, you will be able to *feel* the bass as it was originally intended and understand why these lines are so great. This should build your self-esteem and confidence and allow you to play with attitude and authority.

I felt the need to write this bass book because I have been frustrated by inaccurate transcriptions in previous publications. As an educator, I feel it is my duty to present the facts (or the music) as it really went down so aspiring bassists can hear and finally learn what the masters of R&B bass really played. Future generations fear not. You will be learning the true bass lines if you master the tunes in this book.

It is my hope and wish that you will gain a more profound appreciation and understanding of the R&B bass style from this book. I've chosen classic tunes that will hopefully excite and inspire you to deepen your groove. Every bass player becomes a better bass player if he/she can play R&B. If you can groove, every style of music benefits; it's a win/win situation. And then we all benefit.

Groove on,

Glenn Letsch

TECHNIQUE AND THEORY PRIMER

Rhythm and blues is not a particularly complicated style as far as music theory. However, as an R&B bassist, you need to be familiar with specific diatonic scales and arpeggios as well as commonly-used blues scales and patterns. More importantly, you need to be able to implement all of these routines with quickness and authority.

The rhythmic aspect of playing R&B does require a sophisticated level of technical ability. It is often said the best technique is that which is not noticed. If your technique is not distracting in any way to the listener, then he or she can completely focus on the music itself.

So, rather than present a series of rhythmic routines to practice that may be boring, we will discover R&B rhythm by jumping into the pool, so to speak. That is to say, let's examine and learn to play many classic R&B songs. We'll start with the less-demanding ones and gradually build our chops. As we get better, we can work through the more demanding ones, one by one. Ultimately, if you can play comfortably through all the tunes in this book, you will have a strong command of the R&B genre.

Before we jump into that R&B pool, let's review some essential technique and music theory concepts.

PLUCKING HAND

Fingerstyle

For the most part R&B is played *fingerstyle*. When specific songs in this book suggest otherwise, like picking or slapping, the specific technique will be reviewed at that time. Use your index and middle fingers to pluck each string. Rest the thumb against the pickup when plucking the low E string. When moving to play the A, D, and G strings, rest the thumb against the low E string. Begin plucking with the middle finger and *alternate* it with your index finger.

Rake

The only time you should not alternate is when you are moving from a higher string (like the G) to a lower string (like the D). The finger to pluck the last note on the higher string then *naturally* falls into position against the next lower string, ready to pluck the first note on that string. This is called a *rake*.

FRETTING HAND

When playing this style, the fretting hand will usually be in one of two positions: the *four-fret stretch*, and the *three-fret stretch*.

The Four-Fret Stretch

This hand position makes scales, arpeggios (chord tones), and melodic phrases easier because you can reach most of the notes without shifting. Drop your thumb to the midpoint along the back of the neck. The thumb should be almost opposite the middle finger. This makes it easier to stretch all four fingers over four frets. If this is difficult, your thumb is probably peeking over the top of the fingerboard. Lower it!

The Three-Fret Stretch

The three-fret stretch helps us to *groove*. The name is slightly deceiving, because it may suggest that we only use three fingers. However, we're actually spreading all four fingers over three frets. I call this "the cup" or "bunch of bananas." It is the best fretting-hand fingering technique for groove bass playing because:

- Three frets is just about the width of your four fingers, so it's a natural hand position.
- The "bunch of bananas" helps mute strings you are not playing and articulate the notes you are playing (it allows a bit more punch).
- It allows for economy of motion.
- It puts less stress on hand and wrist joints.

STRINGS

You may want to consider flatwound or tapewound strings for R&B. This is not to say you can't use roundwound strings; you can obviously use whatever you want. But some of that old-fashioned, thumpin' tone was created on Fender Jazz and Precision basses of the early 1960s. Those basses had tonal characteristics not often heard in today's instruments. If you want to get a sound like you hear on all those great songs, consider the type of string you put on your bass.

Also, you may want to stuff a small piece of foam rubber under your strings right next to the bridge. This will cut down on sustain and make your bass sound a bit more percussive. Some old Fenders came with foam attached to their huge chrome bridge covers. These chrome "decorations" actually had a functional purpose. Leo Fender wanted his basses to *thump*. He got it right way back when.

SCALES

Please examine and master the following scales and modes before proceeding with the songs in this book. It will only make the learning process in the subsequent chapters more enjoyable, because these incredible songs will actually be easier to play! Pay close attention to the L.H. fingerings next to the notes on the staff: index finger = 1, middle = 2, ring = 3, and pinky = 4.

It might seem odd to jump with the same finger in the pentatonic scale examples, but give it a try. The rhythms sometimes flow more naturally when you navigate up the fretboard with this method. Keep an open mind about it. If you watch some of the R&B greats closely in concert, they will likely employ these fingerings more than the "alternate" fingerings.

Also, when you see the fingering "3,4" you can use the ring and pinky finger as a team or either finger by itself. Whichever you do, try to keep them close together. This encourages the "bunch of bananas" technique to your fretting hand. It keeps you off your fingertips and also helps the fingers to lie down against the strings and mute unwanted sounds.

Major Scale

As simple as this scale is, it is the fountain for all music theory and must be discussed. You must look at the major scale notes as a succession of *intervals*. Each note in the scale is assigned a number name and referenced against the root (in this case C).

C	Root
D	Major 2nd
E	Major 3rd
F	Perfect 4th
G	Perfect 5th
A	Major 6th
B	Major 7th
C	Perfect Octave

TRACK 1

C Major Scale

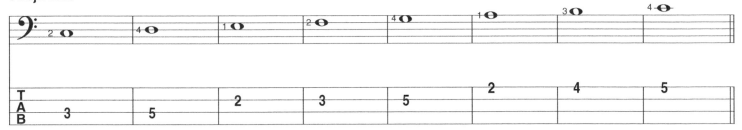

Mixolydian Mode (Dominant 7th Scale)

In order to play a Mixolydian mode, simply play a major scale and flat the 7th (lower by a half step). This is a very popular scale when you want a bluesy, yet major feel. In fact, most young rockers almost invariably play this scale when asked to play the major scale at their first music lesson. So much of today's music utilizes this scale that many listeners' ears are more tuned in at an early age to the ♭7th rather than the more traditional-sounding major 7th (as you'd expect from the "Sound of Music" generation of the 1960s).

C	Root	G	Perfect 5th
D	Major 2nd	A	Major 6th
E	Major 3rd	B♭	Minor 7th
F	Perfect 4th	C	Perfect Octave

TRACK 2

C Mixolydian Mode

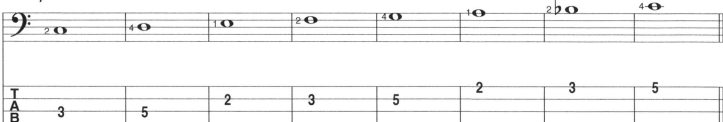

Dorian Mode

To create the Dorian mode, flat the 3rd and 7th of the major scale (lower these notes by a half step). This scale is very popular in R&B. In fact, it is much more often used than the traditional natural minor scale. The blues and R&B often prefer the half step between the major 6th (A) and the flat 7th (B♭), rather than the whole step of the traditional minor scale. It helps retain that honky-tonk feel so popular in blues music. Pluck the C, then rock between the A and B♭ and you will hear for yourself.

C	Root	G	Perfect 5th
D	Major 2nd	A	Major 6th
E♭	Minor 3rd	B♭	Minor 7th
F	Perfect 4th	C	Perfect Octave

TRACK 3

C Dorian Mode

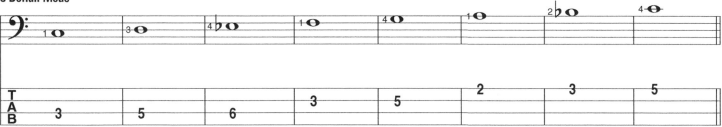

Major Pentatonic Scale

The major pentatonic scale is a five-note version of the major scale consisting of the following:

C	Root	G	Perfect 5th
D	Major 2nd	A	Major 6th
E	Major 3rd	C	Perfect Octave

If you ascend straight up the scale, you are playing the opening guitar line to the Motown hit "My Girl" by the Temptations. If you had to pick the five most useful notes of the major scale, they would be the notes of the major pentatonic scale. Many great bass lines use this scale.

TRACK 4

C Major Pentatonic Scale

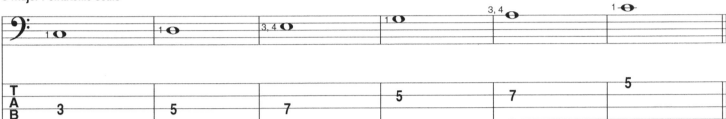

C Major Pentatonic Scale (alternate fingering)

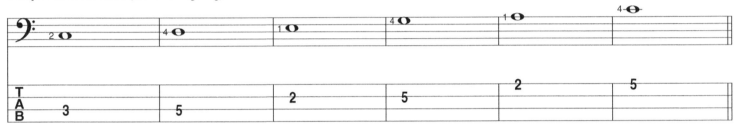

Minor Pentatonic Scale

The minor pentatonic scale is a five-note version of the minor scale consisting of the following:

C	Root	G	Perfect 5th
E♭	Minor 3rd	B♭	Minor 7th
F	Perfect 4th	C	Perfect Octave

TRACK 5

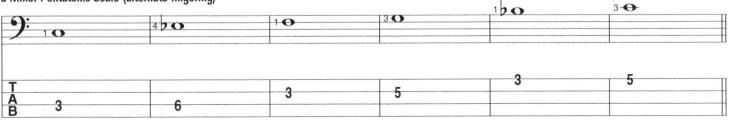

C Minor Pentatonic Scale (alternate fingering)

Major Blues Scale

To make the major pentatonic sound more bluesy, we add a chromatic note (the minor 3rd, E♭) between the major 2nd (D) and the major 3rd (E♮).

C	Root	G	Perfect 5th
D	Major 2nd	A	Major 6th
E♭	Minor 3rd	C	Perfect Octave
E	Major 3rd		

TRACK 6

C Major Blues Scale

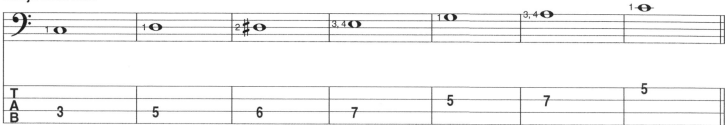

Minor Blues Scale

To make the minor pentatonic sound bluesy, we add a chromatic note (F♯ or G♭) between the perfect 4th (F) and the perfect 5th (G).

C	Root	G	Perfect 5th
E♭	Minor 3rd	B♭	Minor 7th
F	Perfect 4th	C	Perfect Octave
F♯ or G♭	Augmented 4th or Diminished 5th		

TRACK 7

C Blues Scale

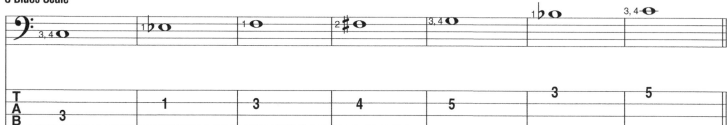

C Blues Scale (alternate fingering)

Altered Major Blues Scale (Popular Version)

This scale is very common yet often ambiguously defined. The great James Jamerson of Motown fame made these notes famous with his stylized rhythmic approach. Anybody can ascend these notes during an R&B chord progression, and everybody has. However, Jamerson was the first to make these notes sound like it was the first time you had ever heard them.

C	Root	A	Major 6th
E	Major 3rd	B♭	Minor 7th
F	Perfect 4th	B	Major 7th
F# or G♭	Augmented 4th or Diminished 5th	C	Perfect Octave
G	Perfect 5th		

TRACK 8

C Altered Major Blues Scale

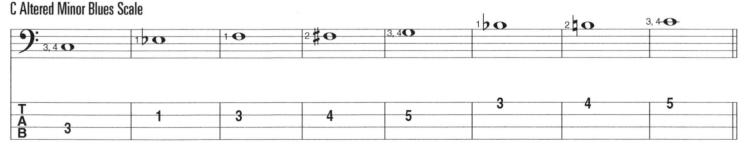

Altered Minor Blues Scale (Popular Version)

This is also common yet often ambiguously defined. It's basically a minor blues scale with a note added (the major 7th) between the minor 7th and the perfect octave.

C	Root	G	Perfect 5th
E♭	Minor 3rd	B♭	Minor 7th
F	Perfect 4th	B♮	Major 7th
F# or G♭	Augmented 4th or Diminished 5th	C	Perfect Octave

TRACK 9

C Altered Minor Blues Scale

C Altered Minor Blues Scale (alternate fingering)

Natural Minor Scale (Aeolian Mode)

To create the natural minor scale, flat the 3rd, 6th, and 7th of the major scale (lower these notes by a half step). This scale is less popular in R&B, but still occasionally used; therefore it is included in this chapter. It is also referred to as simply "the minor scale" or the *relative* minor scale. If you play a major scale starting on its 6th degree to an octave above, you have created that major scale's relative minor scale. The relative minor of C major is A minor. The relative minor of G major is E minor, etc.

C	Root	G	Perfect 5th
D	Major 2nd	A♭	Minor 6th
E♭	Minor 3rd	B♭	Minor 7th
F	Perfect 4th	C	Perfect Octave

TRACK 10

C Natural Minor Scale (Aeolian Mode)

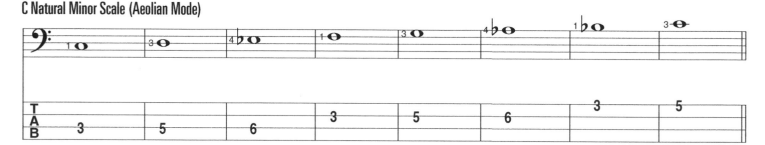

ARPEGGIOS

Being able to outline the chords of a song is an essential skill for an R&B bassist. Following are the most common intervals, arpeggios, and chords used by bass players of this style. Get to know them well as they represent the core backbone of the music.

Major 3rd

3rds are the building blocks of chords. The distance between a root and a major 3rd is two whole steps (four frets on one string).

TRACK 11

Major 3rd

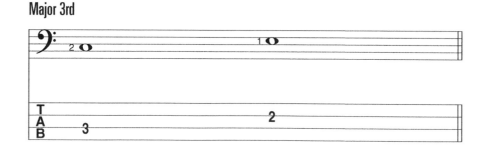

Minor 3rd

The other type of 3rd is a minor 3rd. Together you can create all types of chords by stacking these two intervals in various combinations. The distance between a root and a minor 3rd is one and a half steps (three frets on one string).

TRACK 12

Minor 3rd

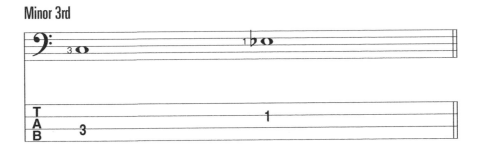

Major Triad

A major triad (*triad* is the name for a three-note chord) consists of a root, major 3rd, and perfect 5th. Alternatively, you can view a major chord as a major 3rd followed by a minor 3rd. It is important to understand these concepts, but it is even more important to be able to *arpeggiate* (play the notes of the chord one at a time) through these notes effortlessly and fluently.

TRACK 13

C Major Triad

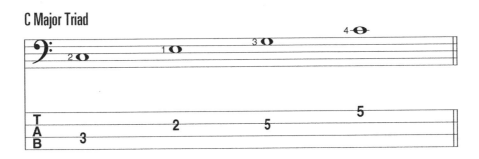

Minor Triad

A minor triad consists of a root, minor 3rd, and perfect 5th. You can also view it as a minor 3rd followed by a major 3rd. (In this respect, it is the opposite of the major chord.) You cannot practice these arpeggios enough. Later in the book you will understand why. But for now, if you do not become fluent with these chord shapes, you will not be able to make these lines groove.

TRACK 14

C Minor Triad

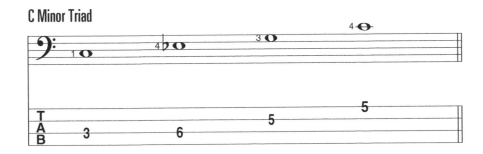

Diminished Triad

A diminished triad consists of a root, minor 3rd, and diminished 5th. You can also view it as a minor 3rd followed by another minor 3rd. The diminished chord is not often used in R&B, but you may come across it occasionally.

TRACK 15

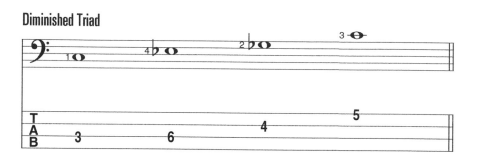

Major 7th Chord

This chord is more popular in jazz than R&B, but like the diminished chord, it just may come up. It consists of a root, major 3rd, perfect 5th, and major 7th. Also, it is defined as a major 3rd, followed by a minor 3rd, followed by a major 3rd.

TRACK 16

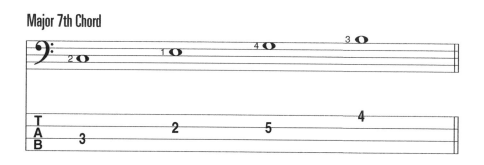

Minor 7th Chord

This chord is often used in R&B. It consists of a root, minor 3rd, perfect 5th, and minor 7th. Also, it is defined as a minor 3rd, followed by a major 3rd, followed by a minor 3rd.

TRACK 17

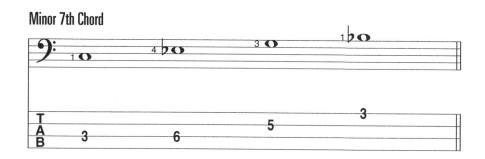

Dominant 7th Chord

This is the most-used 7th chord in R&B. It consists of a root, major 3rd, perfect 5th, and minor 7th. Also, it is defined as a major 3rd, followed by a minor 3rd, followed by a minor 3rd.

TRACK 18

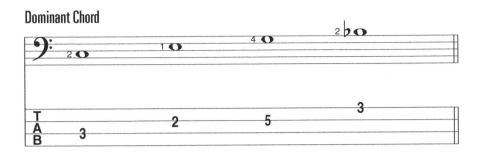

Minor 7♭5 Chord

This chord is rare in R&B, but as a diatonic 7th chord (built off the major scale's 7th note), it needs to be mentioned. It consists of a root, minor 3rd, diminished 5th, and minor 7th. Also, it is defined as a minor 3rd, followed by a minor 3rd, followed by a major 3rd.

TRACK 19

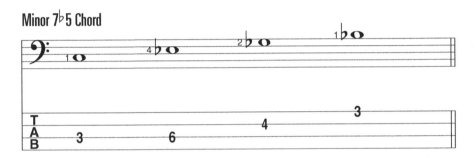

Root—5th—Octave

You will probably work off this chord shape more than any other in all of R&B. It consists of a root, perfect 5th, and perfect octave. Practice this all over the fretboard. Ascend and descend through every conceivable position. You will need three strings to play this. Alternate your fingers on your plucking hand when ascending, and rake one finger across all three strings as you descend. You must execute this pattern correctly or it will sound awkward. A great number of R&B bass lines employ this pattern, so make it automatic in your repertoire.

TRACK 20

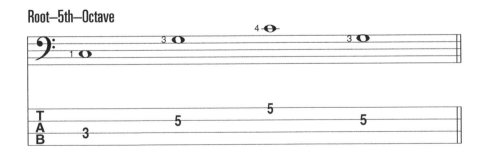

ROOT—5TH—OCTAVE PATTERN

Practice the following example so you can master these *rhythm intervals.* It is very important that you can navigate effortlessly through intervals. Practice slowly at first, and then build up your tempo over time. Be sure your plucking fingers are used exactly as indicated. This will guarantee that you alternate and rake at the appropriate times.

Also, please notice that you alternate your starting finger (middle or index). This will insure that over time you can play these routines *intuitively.* CAUTION: Failure to use the correct plucking fingers can be fatal to your groove!

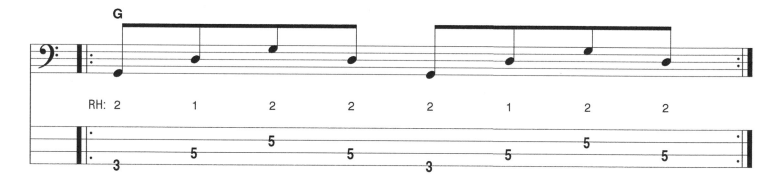

STAND BY ME

Here is one of the first songs that I can remember with a predominantly-featured bass line. It appears to be an upright bass on the recording, released circa 1961. The bass line is symmetrically perfect. I like to think of it as one of those parts that simply cannot be improved upon. It is presented here in its original form and played in the original key of A major. In all likelihood, the bassist was in first position, so the tablature is set to the first four frets of the electric bass. There is the occasional open string that must be dealt with, but that's all right. It will make you a better player if you can control those pesky open strings.

This bass line is built on the I–vi–IV–V chord progression that is so common in R&B. The tune opens with the often-used 5–7–1 walkup—that is to say, the perfect 5th, major 7th, and root of A major (in this case, E–G♯–A). Next is a scalar walkdown to the F♯m, alternating between the root (F♯) and minor 7th (E). Then we move down the scale to D and up to its 3rd (F♯), with a similar move on E, returning to A for measures 7 and 8. The cycle then repeats.

Thumb and Palm Muting

If you approach this song with a technique called *thumb* and *palm muting*, you will capture a sense of tonal mood that will elevate the tune to a higher aesthetic. If I want an upright bass tone, I can come pretty close (as close as an electric can get) with my fretless bass, my thumb, and my palm mute.

Let's begin with the proper position. Rest the fleshy part of the right side of your hand on the bridge of your bass. A good place to start is right behind the saddles that elevate your strings. Relax your four fingers and let them rest either on the pickguard or against the bottom of the G string (not the side you would thumb). Now pluck the low E string with the side of your thumb, allowing your thumb to follow through and come to rest against the A string. Do not go past the A string. Always let your thumb use the next higher string as a backstop. Now pluck the D string, and let your thumb come to rest on the G. When plucking the G string, your thumb may touch the side of your fingers.

Depending on how much muting you want to introduce, roll the side of your hand over the saddles and try deadening the strings. Notice the notes begin to mute and get punchy. You will begin to feel more expressive with the nuances. "Stand by Me" sounds terrific with this technique.

Words and Music by JERRY LEIBER, MIKE STOLLER and BEN E. KING
© 1961 (Renewed) JERRY LEIBER MUSIC, MIKE STOLLER MUSIC and MIKE & JERRY MUSIC LLC
All Rights Reserved

KNOCK ON WOOD

"Knock on Wood" (by Eddie Floyd) is one more classic R&B tune made even more special by Donald "Duck" Dunn's solid bass line. The song is in the key of E major and starts with a series of roots through the chord progression. Traditional R&B would often build a chord off the minor 3rd (G♮ in this case), rather than the diatonic major 3rd (G♯). This is an example of a *borrowed chord*. It's temporarily "borrowed" from the parallel key of E minor, but the tonic chord (E) remains a major chord. R&B would often bend the rules this way, but it always seemed to work.

Uncommon Positions

It might be best to play in the general area of twelfth position (refer to the tablature). Then, when you jump to the verse, the upper A octave routine is right next door. This is a 1–6–5–3 "sixth chord" arpeggio and is a very common part to play on bass. However, to play it in the upper register is slightly uncommon. But there is no doubt—the part "jumps out" when played up there. In fact, you must play the A routine of the verse on the middle two strings above the twelfth fret. If you opt to play it on the D and G strings, the notes will not be as powerful. Try it for yourself and see.

Bridge Section

Note the bridge seems to return to classic diatonic chords, where F♯ (the chord built from the major 2nd) and G♯ (the chord built from the major 3rd) are both minor chords. But there's another borrowed chord (C) at the conclusion of the bridge. Because of the repeating horn lines through these chords, it appears like the F♯m, G♯m, and A chords are all part of a modulation process rather than an attempt at a diatonic chord progression. It really doesn't matter for the bass though, as Duck pedals roots to keep the "floor" solid and the tune irresistible.

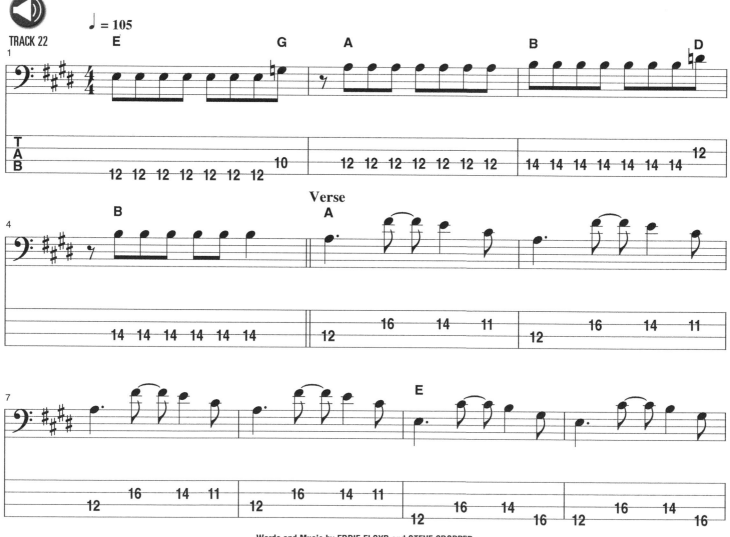

Words and Music by EDDIE FLOYD and STEVE CROPPER
Copyright © 1966 IRVING MUSIC, INC.
Copyright Renewed
All Rights Reserved   Used by Permission

MUSTANG SALLY

Of the numerous renditions, Wilson Pickett's version of "Mustang Sally" has become the standard to which all others are to be compared. Written by Sir Mack Rice, the bass line was performed by Tommy Cogbill.

The bass line, at a casual glance, appears to be a typical box pattern. The "typical box pattern" means the majority of the bass routine is played within the octave box (a three-fret stretch). Roots, 5ths, ♭7ths, octaves, and occasional perfect 4ths are woven together in a repeating pattern. Sometimes playing "in the box" forces you to confine your playing to a generic blues routine. But this is hardly the case here.

Generic Vs. Unique

Interestingly, the classic "Mustang Sally" bass line is one of the most misquoted bass lines in R&B history. I have never heard this bass part played correctly—either by a bar band, or even a newer recorded rendition. The problem is that most players who try to decipher the bass line do not hear the correct notes; they approach the song *generically* rather than *uniquely*. What I mean by this is they try to process the bass line by employing a familiar pattern for their fretting hand (and their ear). This can be a serious mistake. You should always be looking for what makes a song (and the bass line) special and unique. This means that sometimes the notes are not always in familiar places.

Your Ears

A musician's first instrument should be his or her ear. The instrument he or she holds is his/her secondary instrument. If you accept this concept, you must train your ear before you can play your instrument effectively. This is obvious to most of us. We all need ear training, but that is the subject of another book altogether. But for the sake of *feeling* this bass line, let us practice playing and *listening* to half-step intervals. Alternate between the notes C and B repeatedly. Then try *singing* the part as you play it, George Benson style. Be sure to hit the exact pitch so you can feel the note. You need to intuitively feel how *different* these notes sound.

Next, alternate and play a whole step between C and B♭ repeatedly and sing along. Go back and forth between the whole- and half-step intervals until you can hear how different they sound. They aren't even close, are they? If you understand my point, then you are ready to learn how to play "Mustang Sally." It's time to bring the song to life. Rather than lower the bar to bar-band generic, let's raise that bar to studio-musician cool.

Keep in mind that these musicians were brought in to make hit songs because they were the best musicians around. They had diverse musical backgrounds and were monster players with monster chops. They were asked to make these special tracks because they could deliver on their instruments with unique creative energy under pressure in the recording studio. They avoided sounding generic like it was the bubonic plague.

This classic bass line starts with a simple early country root-fifth approach (C–G, C–G) but with a few very hip twists. The approach tone from the chromatic half step below is introduced (B–C and F#–G), along with a syncopated upbeat feel on the 5th (G) and its chromatic approach tone (F#). Insert the A note as a scalar connector note after the 5th, and you have a routine that goes B–C–F#–G–A–B–C. The A note helps *direct* your ear back toward the root. Lo and behold, you have pure musical magic.

Factor in the rhythmic and harmonic counterpoint of the two guitar parts along with the drum pattern, and you have an undeniable musical hit that sounds as fresh today as the day it came out nearly four decades ago. Did you notice the hammer-on guitar part using the half-step chromatic approach? Maybe that was the catalyst for the bass player's line, or, vice versa. It really doesn't matter. What we do know is that these cats had huge ears. They could feel what worked. Play this song with this heightened sense of musical awareness, and everyone in the joint will be jumpin'—guaranteed.

MUSTANG SALLY

Words and Music by BONNY RICE
Copyright © 1968 Fourteenth Hour Music
Copyright Renewed
International Copyright Secured   All Rights Reserved

I'LL TAKE YOU THERE

"I'll Take You There" was performed by the Staple Singers and written by Alvertis Isbell. Another classic R&B bass line, it is a lesson in economy of hand motion and tasteful fundamental chord theory usage. Using the most ergonomic, economic technique to execute this bass part will provide you with the tools to tackle more demanding lines. Though this bass line *sounds* easy, it is not physically easy at first. But by using proper right- and left-hand technique and practicing these techniques *daily*, it will surely become easy. More importantly, you will soon find more daunting bass lines less challenging as a result of mastering these basic R&B fingering and plucking skills.

Articulation

The verse is played *staccato* (short articulate notes), while the solo section is played *legato* (smooth and connected, with no perceptible spaces of silence between all notes). The two sections are a study in musical contrasts, and both are more effective as a result.

Verse Section

Let's look at the verse first; it is much easier to navigate through. The chord progression is C–F and is played in first position (first finger on fret 1). Refer to the first two measures of notation for proper fretting-hand fingering. Try to keep your fingers from arching up on your fretting hand. Guitarists need to be up on their fingertips, but bassists need not, as we're usually only playing one note at a time. Let your fingers rest against the strings you are *not* playing. This will keep the unused strings silent, and your playing will sound more percussive. At first this will be very difficult to do, but with time and effort, it will become second nature. Just be patient. Enunciate the notes you intend to play with a crisp sense of staccato. Don't pluck too hard, but also don't be too polite, or the notes will not come to life.

Words and Music by ALVERTIS ISBELL
Copyright © 1972 IRVING MUSIC, INC.
Copyright Renewed
All Rights Reserved   Used by Permission

Solo Section

Let's consider the solo next. Again we have the same progression: C–F. This means every four beats the song alternates between C major and F major, and the bass part will be *outlining* each chord. A major chord consists of the root, major 3rd, and perfect 5th of a given major scale. So a C major chord contains C (root), E (major 3rd), and G (perfect 5th). An F major chord contains F (root), A (major 3rd), and C (perfect 5th). This will be of great benefit as we construct our bass line for the solo.

Right from the beginning the bass solo feels *melodic*. This is because it starts not on the root of the chord, but on the 3rd (E). Melodic phrases often begin on harmonic intervals (3rd, 5th, 7th, etc.). If your solo always starts on the root, you might sound like you are about to run up the scale in a "Do–Re–Mi–Fa–Sol–La–Ti–Do" fashion. Starting on other chord tones breaks up the predictability and adds melodic interest. Try it and you will find out for yourself. Notice that by starting the solo on E, an Em harmony is almost implied for the first measure.

Start the solo on the fourteenth fret of the D string with your third finger. Next comes the major 6th (A) at the fourteenth fret of the G string with your pinky. Be sure to start that A with the G grace note one whole step below. You pluck the G and *slur* (with a hammer on) into the A. Next, play that same G again (the perfect 5th of C) at the twelfth fret of the G string with your index finger.

In measure 2, over the F major chord, you will play a descending arpeggio. That is merely a fancy way of stating you will play from the highest note in the chord to lowest, *one note at a time*. Once again there is a grace note to be played. Play the high E grace note at fret 14 of the D string with your ring finger. Then, slur into the F octave at fret 15 with your pinky. Next, play C (perfect 5th) at fret 15 of the A string with your ring finger. Next play the low F (root) at fret 13 of the E string with your first finger.

Most importantly, you will *rake* through all of these notes with one finger of your plucking hand. Actually this rake will begin from the high G (last note played on the C chord in the previous measure). Four notes (one on each string) will have been plucked with one finger on your plucking hand. That is about as economical as you can get!

Now our plan is to move back to a C chord for the second half of the solo. After the octave–5th–root rake (also known as the 8–5–1 rake), shift to F's major 3rd (A) with your third finger. Then, similarly to as you did at the beginning of the solo over the C major chord, play F's major 6th (D) with your pinky. Then slide down with the same finger and play the C (tenth fret, D string). Your are now in position to rake the 8–5–1 intervals of the C chord. The halfway point of the solo phrase concludes with a slide to C's major 6th, A with the third finger, and a double hit on the C concludes the phrase.

For the second ending, the 8–5–1 rake on the C chord is followed by a C repeated in the same register in the next measure, where it serves as the 5th of F. The solo returns to the verse and chorus groove at the end.

So to recap: start and end a solo *not* on a root, but on a chord tone. You will have a phrase that is melodic, harmonic, and easy to follow. This brilliant bass line is a perfect example. Every bass player wants to know how to play this line after just the first time hearing this great song.

TRACK 25

GROOVE ME

"Groove Me" is an R&B classic written and performed by King Floyd. This tune is the essence of funk and R&B because beat 1 is clearly defined with a downbeat note (followed by an upbeat note on the "and" of beat 1). What follows is a series of notes all on upbeats. You had better be counting or you will never know when to nail these notes.

Counting

Do you have difficulty playing bass and tapping your foot at the same time? Do you often play the bass rhythm (instead of the pulse) with your foot as you try to locate the groove? If you cannot keep time with your foot while playing a funky groove, we need to fix that ASAP. First, get a copy of this song (or play the audio example over and over) and have a listen, but do not try to play the tune. Just tap your foot on all the downbeats. Try to be accurate. Notice there are two components: your foot goes down and your foot goes up. When your foot is as high as it will go, you have reached the upbeat (or the "and"). This is the exact halfway point between each downbeat. Knowing and feeling this concept is essential. Many notes occur at this exact moment.

The baseball great Yogi Berra always said, "I can't think and hit at the same time." He's in the Hall of Fame, so he could surely hit. He just felt that hitting was automatic. As a bassist, you need to reach a point at which feeling time and playing are automatic, too. After much practice you will be able to forget about your foot, but it is *always* there marking time.

Try this to get yourself started. Tap your foot for four complete measures, counting out loud "1, 2, 3, 4." Do this several times very slowly. Now do the same thing again, but this time count out loud "1 and 2 and 3 and 4 and." Be sure you sound out "and" as your foot reaches for the ceiling. When you can do this "Yogi Berra" style, you are ready to try it with your bass. You should now be able to lock onto the main riff of "Groove Me."

B Section

For the B section, the chords move up to D major and E major, and here's where the heavy funk kicks in. You will use part of the altered major blues scale that we looked at in the first chapter. It might be difficult to hear exactly what the original bass player is playing on the original version, but it's here for you in the notated example. Notice the tablature for the exact place on the neck.

There are some sixteenth notes to consider here. Refer to the notation for the accurate beat subdivision. Now we are dealing with notes halfway between each downbeat and upbeat. The sixteenth note right after the downbeat is referred to as the "e" of the beat, while the sixteenth note right after the upbeat is referred to as the "a" of the beat.

Actually the trickiest part is the conclusion of the two-measure B section (meas. 21–22). Be sure to use your third and fourth fingers when you "dance" between E and B right at the end. Practice this routine slowly so you can later speed it up and articulate it with authority. Have fun with this one.

Pay attention to the tablature. This tune can be fingered in a three-fret stretch with a few jumps or the four-fret stretch in one position. Normally for funk and R&B, you would opt for the three-fret stretch "bunch of bananas"; however, there is not much time to get back into position for the F# pattern. Also, after the D and E measures, you have to work off B on the E string as there is clearly not enough time to get back to fret 2 (as played during the verse). It will make sense if you follow the tablature recommendations.

TRACK 26

Words and Music by KING FLOYD
Copyright © 1970 (Renewed 1998) Malaco Music Company
International Copyright Secured   All Rights Reserved

I CAN'T HELP MYSELF
(SUGAR PIE, HONEY BUNCH)

"I Can't Help Myself" was written by Holland, Dozier, and Holland for the Four Tops. James Jamerson was the bass player. You can walk into any nightclub on a Saturday night and probably hear a cover band playing "I Can't Help Myself (Sugar Pie, Honey Bunch)." Do you need to know how to play this song? Absolutely.

Dorian Mode

This is a diatonic chord progression. This means the chords are strictly within the key (C major in this case). The progression is C–G–Dm–F–G. The bass line moves from chord to chord with the same ostinato figure. Root–5th–6th–root is a standard bass pattern that is typical for major chords. One might expect the bassist to play a root–5th–minor 7th–root pattern over the Dm (ii) chord; it would have been just fine to do that. However, Jamerson had his own way of creating tension with major-type routines implied over minor chords. This is a perfect example. Upon closer scrutiny, the D–A–B–D major-type bass line is diatonically correct over the Dm chord. This is because the Dm is from the D Dorian mode. Dorian is a minor scale with a ♭3rd and ♭7th. The 6th is major (B) in a D Dorian mode. This allows the D–A–B–D lick to work just fine.

The same repetitive bass part can now be played over each chord of the song, whether the chord is major or minor. The other three chords (C, F, and G) are all major chords, for which the pattern is typical. If you encounter the ii chord in a future song, this pattern *could* conceivably work in the right situation. Your ear will be the final judge. If it sounds good to you, just tell them Jamerson did it and it sounded great!

Words and Music by BRIAN HOLLAND, LAMONT DOZIER and EDWARD HOLLAND
© 1965, 1972 (Renewed 1993, 2000) JOBETE MUSIC CO., INC.
All Rights Controlled and Administered by EMI BLACKWOOD MUSIC INC. on behalf of STONE AGATE MUSIC (A Division of JOBETE MUSIC CO., INC.)
All Rights Reserved   International Copyright Secured   Used by Permission

CISSY STRUT

"Cissy Strut" by the Meters features George Porter, Jr. on bass. This song is not very difficult to execute, but the groove is another classic and the feel is real. There is a nice quarter-step bend that adds to the feel. So, it must be mastered in your quest for R&B proficiency. Think *light swing* because this thing is not straight eighths, but it is not full swing either. Just lean slightly toward a swing feel and you will have it.

A Section

This tune counts nicely in *cut* time. Also, the rhythm is a bit easier to read alla breve (in "cut" or 2/2 time). The main A section riff is a minor 7th chord arpeggio (descending from the octave). Refer to the tablature for the most natural choices for note location. You will execute a quarter-step bend of the E♭ (minor 3rd) up to the blue note. The *blue note* is neither the minor 3rd nor the major 3rd. Rather, it is an ambiguous note in between the two.

Next comes the 5th–6th–root (G–A–C) "walk up with a twist." This is another misquoted lick in a classic tune. I have heard countless times the minor 7th (B♭) played instead of the major 6th (A). The 6th adds more subtlety and character. Big ears are needed to hear these details, so listen up!

The bass concludes the main riff with a high 5th (G) to low 5th (G) rake. This is accomplished with one finger of the plucking hand. Pluck the high G on the D string and rake through the A string, but make sure your "bunch of bananas" is muting the A string completely. This rake is all about percussion, rhythm, and harmony. Percussion is created with the rake of the dead A string. Rhythm comes from the swinging eighth notes through the rake, along with the pickup note (C) that starts the rake. Harmony is created when the bass emphasizes the high and low 5th (G). This routine is way cool.

B Section

The B section is a straight-ahead box pattern based on the root, 5th, ♭7th, and octave three-fret box. Keep the bunch of bananas going here. Just be sure you don't get confused and play ♭7ths when you should play 5ths, and vise versa.

Solo Section

The solo section vamps on C. Here the bass groove is wide and deep. It doesn't have to be complicated, but it does have to be solid. Check it out. It's just roots (C), high and low 5ths (G), and low 3rds (open E). In measure 6, play the major 7th (B) as a leading tone into the tonic (C) for emphasis. Steady as she goes here. When you are forced to play only chord tones (and the occasional leading tone) for your solo accompaniment, you can truly discover what "pocket playing" is all about. The groove is the only thing that matters. Let your bunch of bananas lay down on those strings as your plucking hand strokes them for rhythmic texture. Don't rush your part. Lay that groove like it's a hot muggy night in N'Orlins.

CISSY STRUT

TRACK 28

By ARTHUR NEVILLE, LEO NOCENTELLI, GEORGE PORTER and JOSEPH MODELISTE, JR.

© 1969 (Renewed 1997) SCREEN GEMS-EMI MUSIC INC.
All Rights Reserved   International Copyright Secured   Used by Permission

(I'M A) ROAD RUNNER

"(I'm a) Road Runner" is a Junior Walker tune written by Holland/Dozier/Holland. James Jamerson played bass. The song is in F, and that starts us at first position on the bass. On the electric bass, first position typically refers to hand placement on the fretboard. Place your first finger at the first fret. The song may require a three-fret routine or a four-fret routine, so accommodate the bass line by shaping your hand to the different stretches as discussed in the Technique and Theory Primer.

Personality

This particular bass routine has a strong incessant drive; it never lets up. The notes need to sound the same. It is recommended you try plucking the whole song with one finger. I prefer my second finger, as it is stronger, but others prefer their first. It is personal preference. You may want to "thumb and palm mute" as in "Stand by Me." In any event, try alternating fingers so you can discover for yourself what really sounds best. You will likely come to the same conclusion and opt for a single finger or thumb to play the whole song. It might be a bit more work at first, but it will open your ears to a deeper listen.

You will discover that each song requires its own special feel to make it sound the way it needs to sound. To get that special sound or feel, you might need to pluck with one finger, or your thumb, or a pick. You may want to stuff some foam rubber under your strings near the bridge to cut down on sustain. It is important that your considerations be made on a song-by-song basis. Each song has its own unique personality and you must accommodate that personality with your bass playing.

The intro of "Road Runner" can almost be considered a bass solo. It is front and center. Pay close attention to the tablature for accurate note location on the fingerboard. First position with a three-fret stretch is the call here. You will work from the altered major blues scale, using the open strings to be ever-so-economical with your hand movements. Stay off your fingertips and more towards your finger pads (where your fingerprints are). Keep your fingers down so they are resting on unused strings. If you play this part accurately, your fretting hand will barely appear to move, but the bass line will dance!

Song Form

This tune can be deceptive. It appears simple, but the arrangement surely is not. The trick is to notice each verse has an A section and a B section. A C section (parts of the A section and the B section combined) then takes you to the chorus. You also must be sure how many times each is played. Refer to the notation as all sections are clearly marked.

There are subtle shifts in the bass line during each pass through the verse. Jamerson had a way of never quite playing the same phrase exactly the same twice. This method makes the bass line breathe and never sound boring—no matter how simple the line might appear.

Words and Music by EDWARD HOLLAND, JR., BRIAN HOLLAND and LAMONT DOZIER
© 1965 (Renewed 1993) JOBETE MUSIC CO., INC.
All Rights Controlled and Administered by EMI BLACKWOOD MUSIC INC. on behalf of STONE AGATE MUSIC (A Division of JOBETE MUSIC CO., INC.)
All Rights Reserved   International Copyright Secured   Used by Permission

Chorus

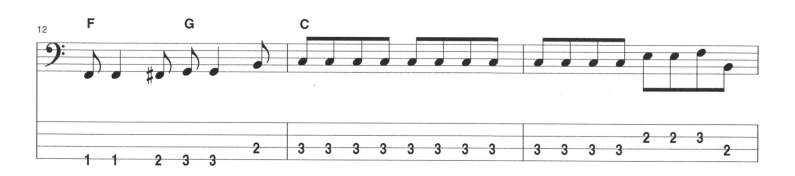

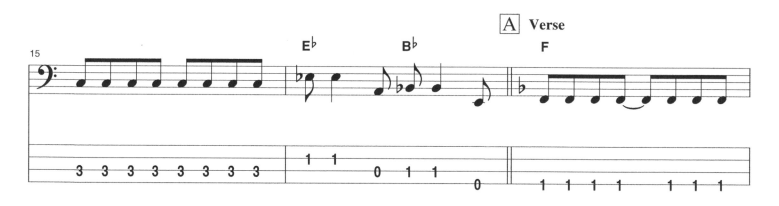

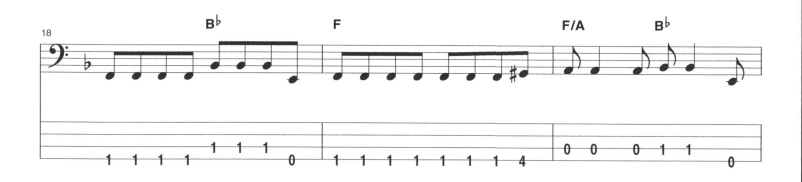

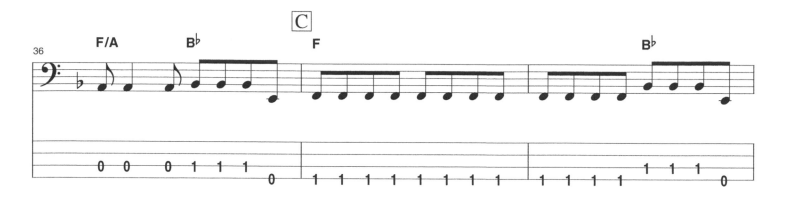

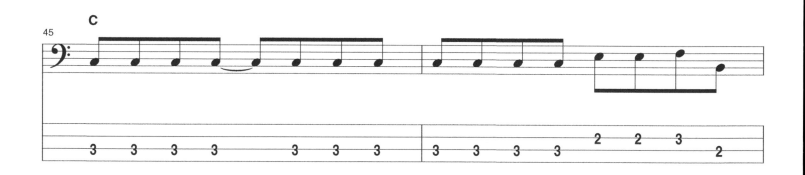

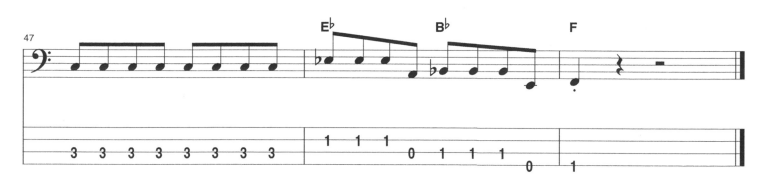

COLD SWEAT, PT. 1

"Cold Sweat" was written by James Brown, and the bass line was played by Bernard Odum. I like to think of this bass line as a yoga mantra: it is a phrase you repeat over and over again. It is intended to clear your mind and center you spiritually. Yes, this bass line is redundant, but it is irresistible—to dancers, listeners, and to the players. The original track goes on for about eight minutes, and the band must have felt like a slow-moving freight train that would not speed up nor slow down. And that is exactly how your bass line should be: locked.

Verse Section

The bass starts out in D for the verse. Though no guitarist is obviously playing chords, the D minor feel can be inferred from the horn line. But even with the "minor" feel of the tune, the bass ignores the minor 3rd of D (F), and bases his routine on a D7 harmony. He starts with a root–octave–♭7th–5th–octave–root phrase in the first measure. He then jumps to the major 3rd (F♯) in the lower register and does a stutter-step chromatic climb up to the 5th (A). He approaches the return to D with the major 7th (C♯), even though the ♭7th (C) was used in the first measure. It appears the bassist preferred the more jazzy chromatic half-step approach tone. This adds a little grease to the bass line and keeps it from sounding too literal. I have often heard this bass line misquoted where bass players assume the ♭7th is used to get you back to D. I suggest you not make this mistake. There is no doubt on the original track that the C♯ is *preferred*.

Bridge Section

Next comes the bridge, and the bass gets very interesting. We move down a whole step to C7, and the bass continues to mimic the D routine, with some slight changes. The bass line now syncopates the first measure and eliminates the sixteenth-note stutter step in the climb to the 5th (G) in the second measure. This is actually a pleasant relief and helps to keep the part from being too repetitive. But something cooler is going on here harmonically. In measure 2 of the bridge the band moves to the IV chord of C (F7), but the bass seems to purposely ignore the change. As a result, his chromatic walkup from low E to G becomes a *harmony* line to what you would normally expect to hear against the F7 chord. It is a 5th below what could have been, and this is very happening. Again, the bassist prefers not to be too *literal* and it creates terrific harmonic tension.

Chorus Section

As the tune moves from the bridge to the chorus (the part of the tune where the title is heard), you *must* count! The song feels as though it stops, but all those unison stabs are actually on the upbeat against a very steady count. The only note on the downbeat is the last note. It is hard to tell this because there is complete silence between the anticipated notes, but there is a steady tempo through this whole section. I have seen bands fail to realize this and play this section *rubato* (with no real pulse). They watch each other for the hits. It ends up sounding and feeling pretty lame. I would recommend you keep time and watch your drummer *imply* silent time so you are all together. This is very, very cool if you pull it off.

COLD SWEAT, PT. 1

TRACK 30

Words and Music by JAMES BROWN and ALFRED JAMES ELLIS
Copyright © 1967 by Dynatone Publishing Co.
Copyright Renewed
All Rights Administered by Unichappell Music Inc.
International Copyright Secured   All Rights Reserved

LICKING STICK—LICKING STICK

"Licking Stick–Licking Stick" was written by James Brown, and the bass line was performed by Tim Drummond. This is a deceptive bass line. Upon first listen, it sounds easy to play. Yes, it *sounds* easy, but don't be fooled. This bass part requires a special touch and quick, agile fingers. Notice the triplet notation at the top of the transcription. This bass line is *swinging*. Also, you must use a very light touch as you pluck so the part can dance. If you play hard, the part will feel stiff.

Easy vs. Correct

The opening lick is an E♭ major chord arpeggio. I have heard this misquoted as an E♭ box pattern lick where the 4th (A♭) is played instead of the major 3rd (G). No question, this makes the riff much easier to play, but it is clearly incorrect. If you play the riff correctly as E♭–G–B♭, then play E♭–A♭–B♭ you will hear for yourself why the G is your only realistic option.

So, if we have to play an E♭ major arpeggio, we must figure out how to do this and keep the groove flowing as we play through the rest of the routine. There are two ways to accomplish this. After playing E♭ with the second finger on your fretting hand and G with your first finger, conventional wisdom would tell you to fret the B♭ with your fourth finger and bridge that finger down to also get the following octave E♭. This is certainly possible. However, consider the third finger as another choice for the B♭. This frees up your pinky to play only the octave E♭.

You can then play the rest of the phrase in the three-fret "bunch of bananas" cup before returning to the E♭ arpeggio pickup. Catching B♭ with your third finger might feel strange at first, but you will soon gain strength and agility through repetition. Experiment with both fingerings and see which works best for you.

Words and Music by JAMES BROWN, BOBBY BYRD and ALFRED ELLIS
Copyright © 1968 by Fort Knox Music Inc., Trio Music Company and Toccoa Industries
Copyright Renewed
International Copyright Secured   All Rights Reserved
Used by Permission

SUPER BAD SUPER SLICK

"Super Bad" was written by James Brown, with Bootsy Collins playing the bass line. The modus operandi is simple: find an irresistible groove and repeat it over and over. Then, go to the bridge (usually the IV chord), find another groove, and repeat that. The conductor (James) signals a return to the first groove with one of his trademark screams. You need but one word to describe this series of artistic events—awesome!

Funky Arpeggio

The main groove for the verse comes right from the D major scale. You'll need to be in the four-fret stretch position for this section. It starts with a root-octave figure followed by a sixteenth-note climb from the 3rd (F#) to the 5th (A). An eighth-note root/low 5th figure immediately follows. You could almost describe this as a "funky arpeggio" because it contains all three notes from the major triad (root, 3rd, and 5th). You can think of the perfect 4th as the "perfect" passing tone. Also, notice the occasional chromatic connector (G#) during the main groove (measures 5, 26, and 32). It helps make the groove *liquid*. It also breaks up the tedium of playing exactly the same riff over and over again.

Bridge Section

The bridge utilizes a manic rendition based loosely on the root–5th–octave pattern from the opening chapter of the book. This is a perfect example of why you must be able to glide up and down through this pattern with ease. The bridge is actually much more involved, but you will not be able to execute this section unless you are *automatic* with the root–5th–octave exercise. Pay very close attention to the fretting-hand fingering in measures 12 and 16 of "Super Bad." These are very *non-generic* licks. Practice them slowly so you can gain effortless control. Learn these bass figures correctly, and it is you who will be "Super Bad."

Words and Music by JAMES BROWN
Copyright © 1975 by Dynatone Publishing Co.
Copyright Renewed
All Rights Administered by Unichappell Music Inc.
International Copyright Secured   All Rights Reserved

Verse

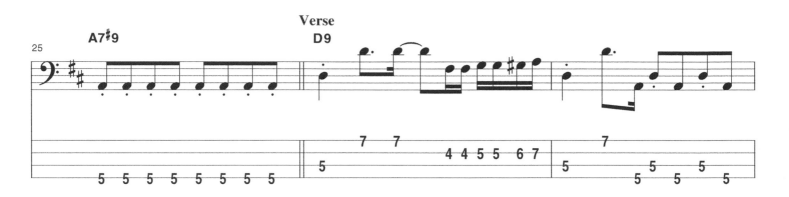

SOUL MAN

"Soul Man" was written by Isaac Hayes and David Porter. Originally performed by Sam & Dave, the bass was handled by Donald "Duck" Dunn. Duck was the house bassist for Stax Records in Memphis, Tennessee. Steve Cropper on guitar, the late Al Jackson on drums, and Booker T. Jones on Hammond B3 rounded out the band. This ensemble, also known as Booker T. & the MGs, played on Otis Redding's tunes as well as a host of others.

Economical Fingerings

The bass to "Soul Man" is the *soul* of the tune. It plays counter to the rhythm guitar but outlines the chords about as fluently as can be done. Duck always had a knack for hitting the nail right on the head when it came to picking just the right bass part. You might be able to find a convenient way to play this tune with some crafty use of open strings, but it's not likely the bass line was approached this way. Proof in point would be the modulation after the bridge. You are stuck in a fretted position in order to pull off the routine in A♭. So, it makes sense that the main body of the song was approached with the same fingering pattern.

This signature riff from the verse can probably be accomplished with a shift to the C on the A string, but you might end up with a bit more string noise than you would like. Consequently, I have notated the transcription with the most economical fretting position, which can be handled nicely in fifth position. What makes this four-fret stretch preferable is the rake down to C on the E string. This deepens the groove. The rake *always* deepens the groove. It is often said the best technique is when it is not noticed at all. The rake makes your "technique" almost undetectable. The listener just hears music, and that is all we ever want.

Contrast and Symmetry

Notice the contrast between the verse and chorus. The bass is very active through the verse, then becomes static by pedaling eighth-note roots during the chorus. This makes the tune feel balanced and symmetrical. The bass needs to breathe and it surely does on this classic tune. This strategy can only help the overall song and its impact on the listener.

The bridge is most interesting, as the key changes from G to E♭. Also, at its conclusion, we modulate again from the key of E♭ to A♭. This lifts the final verse up a half step from the original key of G. Again, work on your shifting so nobody notices your technique as you navigate through the verse groove. Play slowly at first, then slowly increase your tempo until you can comfortably play at the proper tempo.

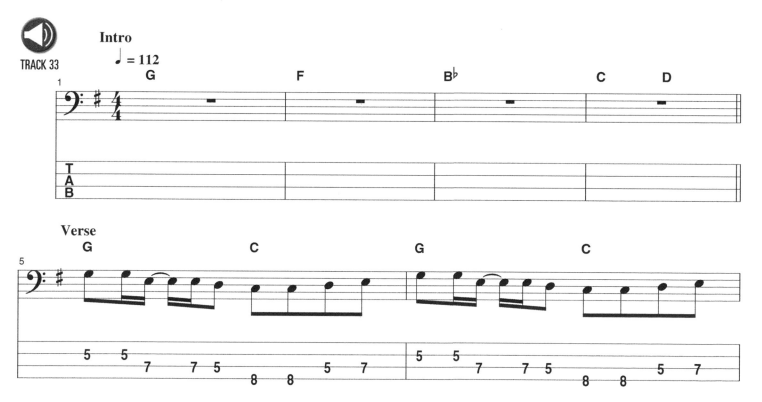

Words and Music by ISAAC HAYES and DAVID PORTER
Copyright © 1967 ALMO MUSIC CORP. and WALDEN MUSIC, INC.
Copyright Renewed
All Rights Reserved   Used by Permission

COOL JERK

"Cool Jerk" was written by Donald Storball, performed by the Capitols, and the bass part was played by Bob Babbitt. The backbeat is fierce and fuels the groove; this song deserves utmost respect. Anyone who played *anything* on this track was at the top of his game, including the tambourine, piano, drums, guitar, and the singers. This song must have given everyone chills listening back in the control room.

The tune is notated *alla breve* ("cut" time) at 83 BPM rather than 166 BPM. Basically, this means that 4/4 time becomes 2/2 time. You count 1–2 where the 1 and 3 normally would be in common time (4/4). This helps you to lock in so you don't have to count at a frantic pace.

Flat Keys

"Cool Jerk" is in the key of E♭. One might expect that to be a hindrance for an electric bass tuned to low E. However, the uniqueness of a high root (E♭) on the bass played against a piano capable of low E♭ support actually widens the overall sonic feel. Plus, consider the sonic impact of the key of E♭ versus the key of E. It was no accident many of the great Motown tunes were in flat keys. Of course, writing on a piano has its advantages when you can play on all those black keys. Many of those songs feature horn parts, which are flat-key instruments. Those keys also just *sound* great. There is an edginess and brightness those keys offer a tune, and that is a big part of why they chose to record in those keys. I wouldn't change anything about this tune.

Verse Section

The bass works off the dominant 7th chord to create a verse groove. The root (E♭) jumps down to the low major 3rd (G) then climbs chromatically to the 5th (B♭)—à la the altered major blues scale. Then it jumps up to the ♭7th (D♭) and back to the high root (E♭). Refer to the tablature for best fingering location.

B Section

The B section moves to the iii chord (Gm) and vi chord (Cm). Then, it jumps to the IV chord (A♭) for a "funky arpeggio" (A♭, C, and E♭) that includes a chromatic climb between the 3rd (C) and the 5th (E♭) followed by a dance between the 5th (E♭) and high root (A♭). Next comes the V chord (B♭), where the bass mimics the routine played on the IV chord but concludes to the low root (low B♭). Opting for the low B♭, Babbitt knows this has stronger impact and acts as an exclamation point as his routine concludes.

This bass line grooves hard. As you play, *feel* the backbeat emphasized on the original recording by the snare drum, tambourine, handclaps, and guitar. Your part will really swing if you key off these instruments. Remember, your first instrument is your ear, and then comes your bass. That is what helps make you a more soulful musician. You must *listen* first, and then play.

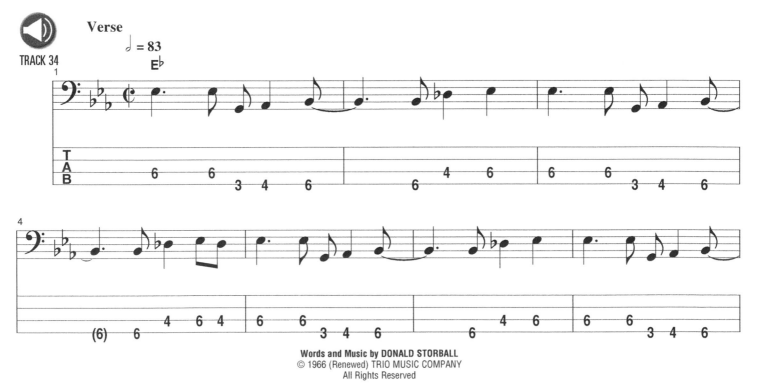

Words and Music by DONALD STORBALL
© 1966 (Renewed) TRIO MUSIC COMPANY
All Rights Reserved

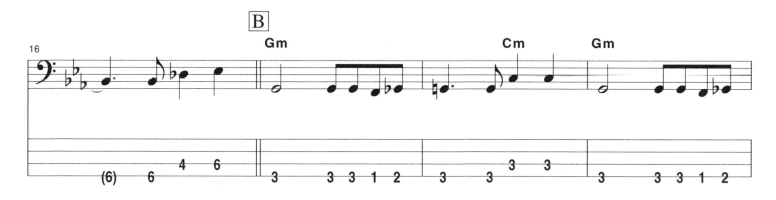

RESPECT

Fender Basses

"Respect" was recorded by Aretha Franklin, written by Otis Redding, and featured Jerry Jemmott on bass. This tune is great. Part of its allure came from the bass pulsing through the speakers of a 1960s tube car radio. The vibe was undeniable. An old Fender bass was used, with flatwound strings. Well, it wasn't old then; in fact, it was brand new. But little has been done over the years to improve the tone of a bass. Back in the early days, the chrome bridge cover was probably left on the bass—for good reason. There was a piece of foam glued to the roof of the bridge cover. When it was placed over the strings, it acted as a mute and increased the percussiveness of the bass. That was all part of the classic Fender bass tone.

Years later, bassists would buy Fenders thinking they would get that sound, but the newer ones came without chrome cover plates, and hence no string mutes. Additionally, modern basses were being strung with roundwound strings. This increased sustain and was good for rock 'n' roll songs and slapping, but it was not so good if you wanted that classic warm, punchy R&B thang.

6ths

This bass line goes down as a must-learn for all aspiring groove masters. The tune is in the key of C and, interestingly, is full of dominant 7th chords. R&B loves dominant 7th chords, but this bass line doesn't hit many 7ths. The bass is more concerned with 6th intervals, which are typical for supporting simple major chords. Therein lies the attraction of the bass line: it is not too literal. The major 6ths come close to the dominant 7ths just enough to "tickle" the harmonic structure. And it works. You probably couldn't get away with doing this if they were minor chords. Typically, you would have to substitute the minor 7th for the 6th, except in rare situations.

The tune opens on the chorus groove. Notice there is a rhythmic contrast between measures. Measure 1 bounces steadily between eighth and sixteenth notes, but measure 2 is full of "upbeat" eighth notes. Consequently, this two-measure phrase breathes. Note that the verse has the same alternating rhythmic treatment.

Clearly, the bass opts for major 6ths to create its routine during the verse and chorus as discussed above. The bass does acknowledge the dominant 7th chord during the transition from verse to chorus. Here, the bass plays the ♭7th (E♭) when it descends from F7 to the C7. It just wouldn't sound cool to hit the diatonic E♮. These cats just knew what was cool.

Contrast and Mood

In contrast to the verse and chorus, the bridge straightens out the chordal and scalar structure, as it opts for roots and 5ths. However, notice it is quite busy rhythmically. This keeps it from dragging. The key shifts from C major to E major, and the F♯m7–B7 progression acts as a ii–V cadence in E. The G7 at the end of the bridge leads the following verse back into the original key of C. Typically, a bridge is a study in contrast from the rest of the tune, and this bridge is no exception. The contrast is most effective when the verse and chorus return like a breath of fresh air.

If you listen closely to the intro and choruses on the original recording, you will hear that the guitar is barely audible as it doubles the bass line. During the verse, the guitar drops out and the bass is left alone to drive the groove. The verse seems more haunting as a result. Most people will not consciously hear this; however, the listener responds on a subconscious level as well, aesthetically feeling the change in *mood*. The chorus has more edge when the guitar subtly doubles the bass line, while the verse mood feels more isolated and haunting when the bass is left to lilt along by itself.

TRACK 35   **Intro**

Words and Music by OTIS REDDING
Copyright © 1965 IRVING MUSIC, INC.
Copyright Renewed
All Rights Reserved   Used by Permission

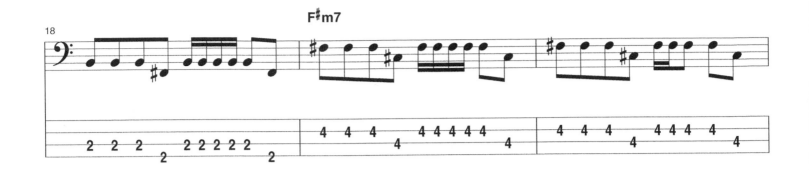

SIGNED, SEALED, DELIVERED I'M YOURS

The classic version of "Signed, Sealed, Delivered I'm Yours" was recorded by Stevie Wonder. Bob Babbitt executed the bass line masterfully. There have been other versions attempted, but none come close to the Stevie Wonder version.

All About the 1

It has been often said that funk is "all about the 1." That means the first beat of the measure has to be clearly stated by the bass and drums. Once "the down of 1" has been played and made obvious to the listener, the funk can begin. Typically this technique revolves around a two-measure phrase, where beat 1 of measure 1 is made very obvious. The remainder of the phrase *gets the funk*.

Subtleties and Nuances

The first thing you should notice about this song is the rhythmic pattern once the verse kicks in: the "and" of beat 4 is accented each time with the new chord change. The kick drum pattern is more deliberate, clearly defining the down beats. This creates a wonderful sense of tension between the drums and bass that flat-out works. If the bass copies the kick drum pattern verbatim, the interplay between the kick and the bass disappears. Just as much as it is important for the bass to lock with the kick, it needs to *not* lock with the kick at strategic rhythmic moments. The bass *implies* the feel of the kick drum with the staccato notes, as it plays *around* the drums. Pay particular attention to this feel during the verse and chorus routines. Listen to the track and refer to the notation and tablature for specifics. It does make a difference if you pay attention to these kinds of details. Subtleties and nuances elevate a performance from "good" to "whoa!"

With that said about playing off the kick drum pattern, you can also lock closer if you pay attention to the notated staccato notes in the transcription. It makes the bass *feel* better. Speaking of feel, don't miss the bluesy quarter-step bend on the A♭ during the intro figure and its repetitions. This is another subtle touch that adds weight to this classic bass line. Of course, the tones of the bass and the bass drum are absolutely gorgeous. This can only help as the rhythm section *sells* the groove to us fortunate listeners.

Glory Hole

The turnaround the bass employs right before the chorus (measures 19–20) is one on the hippest routines a bass player can pull off. Typically the last two measures of a verse, chorus, or bridge can be a *glory hole*, just begging for a bassist to show his stuff. If you have an idea for a terrific two-measure routine, this is the place to make your statement. Pay close attention to the notation and tablature to make sure you accurately nail this classic riff. Hopefully this lick will inspire you to come up with your own moments of bass glory.

SIGNED, SEALED, DELIVERED I'M YOURS

TRACK 36

Words and Music by STEVIE WONDER, SYREETA WRIGHT, LEE GARRETT and LULA MAE HARDAWAY
© 1970 (Renewed 1998) JOBETE MUSIC CO., INC., BLACK BULL MUSIC and SAWANDI MUSIC
c/o EMI APRIL MUSIC INC. and EMI BLACKWOOD MUSIC INC.
All Rights Reserved   International Copyright Secured   Used by Permission

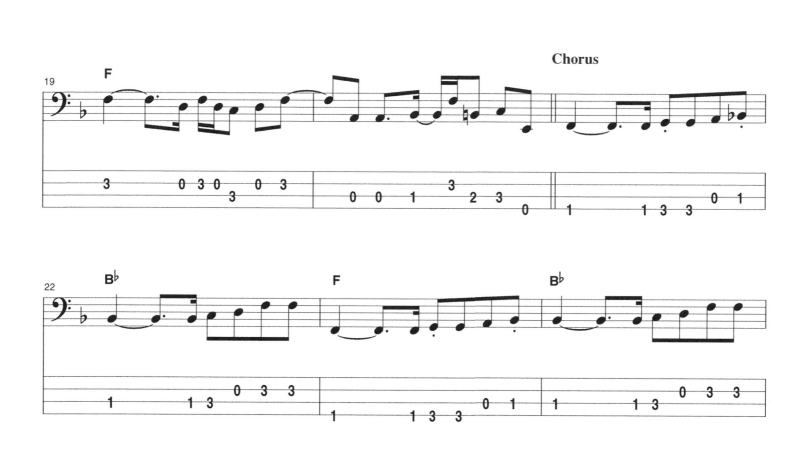

Chorus

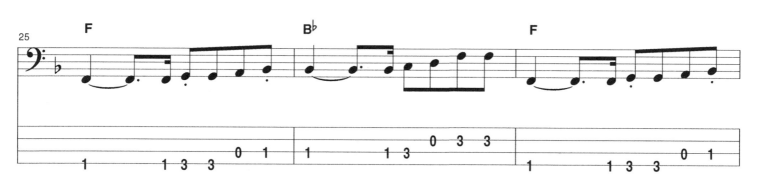

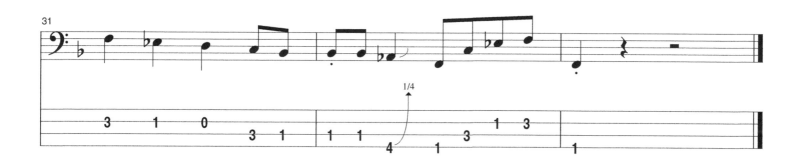

GOOD TIMES

The late, great Bernard Edwards created this powerful R&B line with the band Chic. Used later as the source of "Rapper's Delight," it has become an instantly recognizable bass line. Every student I've ever had lights up when he or she hears it. Everyone wants to learn it, so it's a must in this book.

Dorian Mode

Before we jump right in, we'll examine some of the scales used to create this classic line. Let's take the Dorian mode and funk it up. To review, the Dorian mode is a type of minor scale derived by starting a major scale on the 2nd note and playing to an octave above that note. The key signature for "Good Times" shows the key of D major. Here is the D major scale (D–E–F♯–G–A–B–C♯–D).

D Major Scale

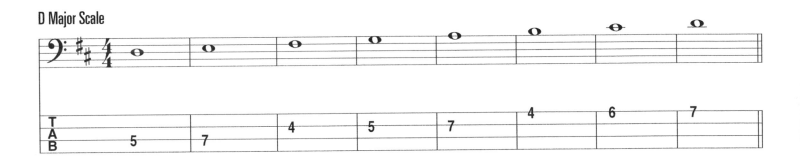

Now play the notes of the D major scale, but start and end on E. You end up with the E Dorian mode (E–F♯–G–A–B–C♯–D–E).

E Dorian Mode (at middle E on the bass)

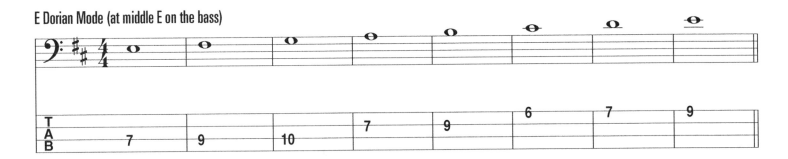

Now let's drop the E Dorian mode down an octave and start from low open E.

E Dorian Mode (at open E)

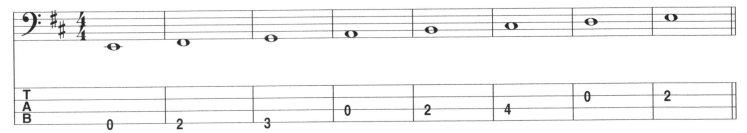

Intervals

You should be thinking *intervals* when you play this mode (number names for distances between notes). There are two definitions for every mode. You must think what interval of the major scale the mode starts on. For instance, the Dorian mode starts on the 2nd. This is the macrocosmic definition, because you relate the scale back to the key from which it is derived (E Dorian is the D major scale starting on the 2nd scale degree).

Here's the microcosmic definition. Look at this E Dorian mode as a kind of E scale. Take the E major scale and flat the major 3rd and the major 7th. You now have half-step (one-fret) intervals between the major 2nd and minor 3rd and between the major 6th and the minor 7th. The Dorian mode is a bluesy minor scale. Hit E, then play C# and D, and this will be obvious to you.

Now climb up this scale and consciously think root, major 2nd, minor 3rd, perfect 4th, perfect 5th, major 6th, minor 7th, and perfect octave. Try to remember what the intervals sound like and what they look like. When you are in E Dorian, you *visualize* the intervals as well as hear them. In other words, you know where the notes are on the fingerboard, and you know what the notes sound like.

Chic Technique

Think E Dorian and you are ready to play the chorus bass line to "Good Times." It is very percussive, so make those low E notes short and crisp (note the staccato dots in the notation). When the band moves to the A7 chord, it is absolutely essential that you rake down to the A string with the same finger. DO NOT pluck the open A with a different finger, or you will lose the feel and the groove will die.

For the A7 the bass plays a classic honky-tonk piano line that includes the major 6th (F#) and minor 7th (G). The raking is quick, so take your time to sort through it before you bring it up to speed. Don't forget to be as economical as possible with your plucking fingers. Be sure to use the same finger when going from the D string back to the A string.

On the A7 chord, be sure to keep your fretting-hand fingers in the "bunch of bananas" shape. If you do not, harmonics will start chiming out of nowhere. To keep these to a minimum, you must rest unused fingers behind your fretting finger. This will keep those chimes nearly undetectable. Pay attention and listen to these details; the more you address subtleties and nuances, the deeper your playing gets.

If you think of Em7 to A7 as a ii–V chord progression, you may be correct. "Good Times" features a diatonic ii–V chord progression in the key of D. The parent key is D, but E is the tonal center of the song, therefore, the progression sounds more like i–IV in the key of E Dorian.

Enunciate and Articulate

The "Good Times" verse groove is a slightly more simplified, yet very effective bass line. It pulses chord roots, deftly bouncing off the ♭7th to the octave, followed by a rake to low E. The move to the next chord (A7) climbs via the ♭3rd up to the A chord root. Crisp and precise technique makes this bass line continue to control the song's rhythmic direction. Be sure to strive for more *control* over your bass. Take your time so the notes are always clearly *enunciated* and *articulated* in their volumes, attacks, and cutoffs. Gradually build up your tempo day by day so the control remains intact as you increase tempo. Only then will the part lie in the pocket exactly as you imagined it could.

GOOD TIMES

TRACK 37

Words and Music by NILE RODGERS and BERNARD EDWARDS
Copyright © 1979 Sony/ATV Songs LLC and Bernard's Other Music
All Rights on behalf of Sony/ATV Songs LLC Administered by Sony/ATV Music Publishing, 8 Music Square West, Nashville, TN 37203
International Copyright Secured   All Rights Reserved

BERNADETTE

"Bernadette" was written by Holland/Dozier/Holland and performed by the Four Tops. The bass line is James Jamerson's. This song is no walk in the park. There is a reason it is one of the final three tunes in this book: it is very demanding. You will need all the skills you have mastered to this point. You must be adept at rapid-fire arpeggios and complicated funk rhythms. If you want to sound credible playing "Bernadette," you must also be comfortable playing in a demanding key like E♭. The good news is you can do it. If you have faithfully studied the previous tunes and theory work presented to this point, you are ready to tackle one of the baddest tunes of all time.

Flat Keys

I once spoke to the great Bob Babbitt (bassist on "Cool Jerk" and "Signed, Sealed, Delivered I'm Yours") about the classic Motown tunes being in flat keys like E♭, A♭, D♭, etc. He told me the writers found it easier to compose in flat keys (just hit the black keys on the piano). But more importantly, they felt the flat keys *sounded* better. And they were right. "Bernadette" really catches your ear in the key of E♭, but it might not have the same impact in E or even D.

Take It Slow

There's a lot going on. You will need to practice this song very slowly to get the feel of the arpeggios during the chorus (starting at measure 3). Proceed slowly so you can burn the routine into muscle memory. Make sure you play the routine in measure 6 correctly. This lick has been misquoted consistently over the years. When you lock in with the recording, this lick will *feel* amazing.

The verse can be tricky. Pay particular attention to the second measure, where the bass line jumps from B♭ (A string, first fret) down to F then low open E before climbing back to D♭ via B and C. It may seem these notes come from left field, but they truly sound incredible in context. Once again, here lies another misquoted lick by previous transcribers. I have never heard anyone get it right. It is a terrific lick and is the essence of Jamerson's style—*never* generic.

Jamerson could be crafty. He knew how to be melodic and interesting by avoiding the diatonically *correct* notes at clever moments. As tough as these parts appear, you will find they are very playable because they come from deep within the groove.

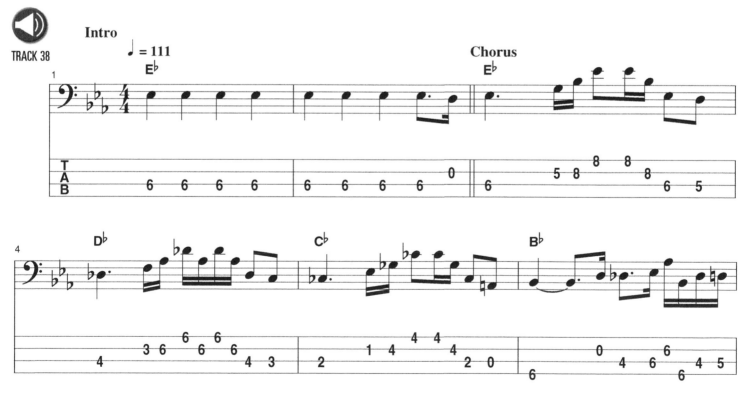

Words and Music by BRIAN HOLLAND, LAMONT DOZIER and EDWARD HOLLAND
© 1967 (Renewed 1995) JOBETE MUSIC CO., INC.
All Rights Controlled and Administered by EMI BLACKWOOD MUSIC INC. on behalf of STONE AGATE MUSIC (A Division of JOBETE MUSIC CO., INC.)
All Rights Reserved   International Copyright Secured   Used by Permission

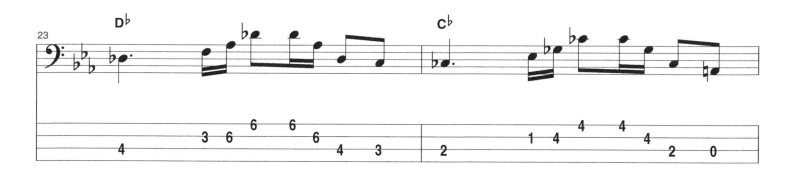

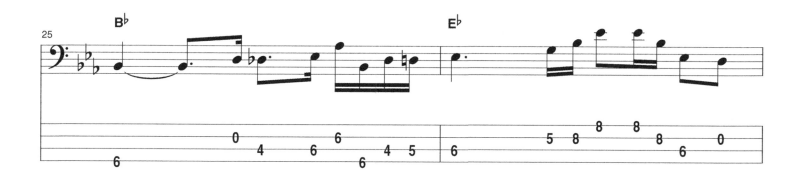

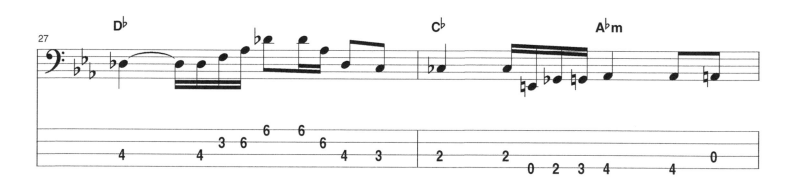

FOR ONCE IN MY LIFE

This is one of the more advanced bass lines in this book. In fact, it might be the toughest of all. That is all the more reason to master it. In 1968, Stevie Wonder released the most interesting version of "For Once in My Life" from a bass player's perspective. Ron Miller and Orlando Murden wrote it, and the great James Jamerson makes the tune with his inventive and relentless bass lines. To this day it is one of the most demanding bass lines to play.

Winking Not Chasing

Beyond its technical difficulty, it is a brilliant piece of bass playing for its sheer musicality. The chords are moving every two beats, but the bass never sounds like it is "chasing the chords." Rather, it sounds like the bass is playing "through the chords" much like an accomplished soloist would. The bass player should not always feel compelled to outline all the defining tones of each chord. Rather, if you concern yourself with propelling the song forward with tasteful rhythm and a "passing wink" at the individual chords' details, the bass line will seemingly have more vision.

Specifically speaking, notice the bass line does not incorporate the stand-out pitches of the F+ chord (the C#) or the F6 chord (the D). Not until the F#°7 does the bass actually arpeggiate the chord. As a result, the bass line "breathes" in the first measure of the tune and delivers the chordal details in measure 2. Thereafter, we see this alternating approach of playing past the chord and occasionally outlining it. At other times the chord tones are downright ignored, as in the F+ chord in measure 16 where the perfect 5th (C) is used instead of the augmented 5th (C#). It almost doesn't matter because the bass line is so fluid and the notes go by so fast. It keeps the bass line from becoming too literal. You have to know when this approach works, but more importantly, you have to know when it won't work. Studying this tune and making it a goal to master will aid you in acquiring the musical wisdom of knowing when to push (and when not to push) the harmonic envelope.

Make sure you practice this song very slowly so you can gain control of your instrument. There are some very good computer software programs that actually slow down a tune while maintaining the original key and pitch. This can be an effective practice tool.

Artificial & Natural Damping

Refer to the tablature, because first position is essential in making this tune feel, play, and sound right. Consider putting flatwound (or tapewound) strings on your bass, or maybe getting a piece of foam rubber to shove under your strings near the bridge. That will make your bass punchier and cut down on sustain. It will also give you more control over the open strings. The open G will sound pretty good with some foam under it. You will be able to use it as well as open D and open A. This will keep you in first position and relax your groove.

That said, getting control of open strings *without* the help of foam is crucial. In fact, you should practice with and without foam under your strings. Additionally, your fretting hand needs to "lay down" on the strings to damp them. This will come after logging hours, days, weeks, and months of practice. Be patient; Rome wasn't built in a day. Neither is funk mastery. Be assured, if you put in the effort, you will reap the reward.

Similarly, your plucking hand needs to utilize unused fingers to help damp vibrating strings. Your thumb should rest on the E string when you play on the D string to avoid any sympathetic vibration when you strike middle E. Similarly, your pinky should rest on the A string when you strike A on the G string. You must listen for unintended vibration from any and all strings and eliminate it. Later, when you reinsert the foam piece under your strings, your performance will sound amazing!

FOR ONCE IN MY LIFE

Words by RONALD MILLER, Music by ORLANDO MURDEN
© 1965 (Renewed 1993) JOBETE MUSIC CO., INC. and STONE DIAMOND MUSIC CORP.
All Rights Controlled and Administered by EMI APRIL MUSIC INC. and EMI BLACKWOOD MUSIC INC.
All Rights Reserved   International Copyright Secured   Used by Permission

WHAT'S GOING ON

Marvin Gaye originally recorded "What's Going On," and the song was written by Al Cleveland, Marvin Gaye, and Renaldo Benson. James Jamerson played the bass. As the story goes, when he returned home after the session, he told his wife he had just recorded the greatest bass part of his career. That may very well be the case. It is the culmination of everything his bass playing was about: deep groove, melodic drive, and rhythmic virtuosity. Therefore, it is the final classic R&B tune presented in this book.

The notation and tablature is presented along with the track for you to hone your chops on this. This transcription is very accurate to Jamerson's original bass track. As with the other tricky Jamerson performances (see "Bernadette" and "For Once in My Life"), this transcription captures the subtlety and nuance not previously published.

Connector Notes

Pay particular attention to the use of the open A "connector notes" in measures 7, 12, 16, 18, 24, and 38. This is brilliant stuff. When you play the part along with the original recording, your bass will "disappear" right into the song because these *are* the subtle details that separate Jamerson's genius from others. At first glance, some of the notes almost seem like wrong notes. They may press the harmonic envelope, but they also economize your left- and right-hand movements so you can sink deeper into the groove. In measure 20 the E♯ chromatic approach tone into the F♯ is perfect in its own way. Measure 22 employs the major 3rd of B (D♯) as measure 23 employs the major 3rd of E (G♯).

The bridge begins in measure 27 with a subtle shift in groove to a light swing. There is also an interesting nod to the major 9th of A (B) on the "e" of beat 3.

R&B Mastery

Start practicing this tune at an easy tempo with your ultimate goal being to attain ♩=100 with total confidence and conviction. There will be a deep sense of accomplishment when you can float through this tune, and the groove feels a million miles wide. It will mean one thing: you are a deep-groovin' R&B bass player. If you can play this tune the way it was intended, you can play anything.

Words and Music by MARVIN GAYE, AL CLEVELAND and RENALDO BENSON
© 1970, 1971, 1972 (Renewed 1998, 1999, 2000) JOBETE MUSIC CO., INC.
All Rights Controlled and Administered by EMI APRIL MUSIC INC. and EMI BLACKWOOD MUSIC INC. on behalf of JOBETE MUSIC CO., INC. and
STONE AGATE MUSIC (A Division of JOBETE MUSIC CO., INC.)
All Rights Reserved   International Copyright Secured   Used by Permission

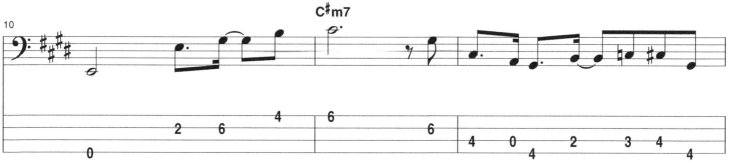

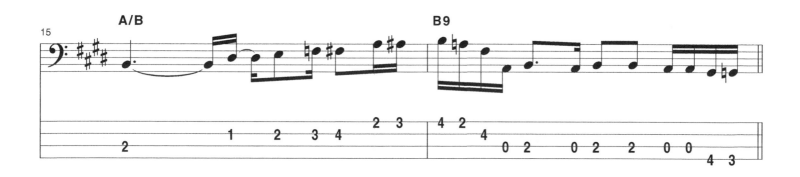

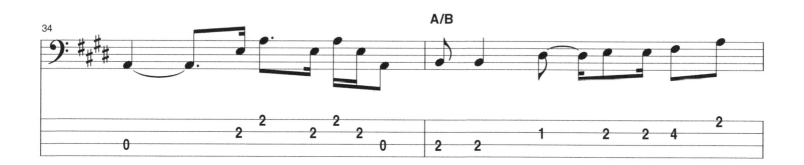

That's it. You've successfully made it through this book, and you've hopefully gained a new command and appreciation for the R&B style. Congratulations! May you groove hard as you journey through your bass-playing career.

ABOUT THE AUTHOR

Glenn Letsch's musical career has spanned over thirty years. As a professional bassist, he has recorded countless albums and toured worldwide. He has graced the concert stage with the likes of Robin Trower, Gamma, Montrose, Gregg Allman, Jonathan Cain, Neal Schon, and many others.

His acclaimed instructional video *Bass Guitar: The Lowdown with Glenn Letsch* (Hot Licks Videos) was rated A+ by *Bass Player* magazine. His first book, *Bass Lessons with the Greats* was hailed by *Bass Player* magazine as "the best instructional text since *Standing in the Shadows of Motown*."

His next book, *Glenn Letsch's Bass Masters Class* is a perennial strong seller for Hal Leonard Publishing, as is his follow-up, *Bass for Beginners: The Complete Guide*. Glenn also has played bass for the top rated *The Sims* computer games. *The Sims* series is the #1 selling computer game in the world today.

Glenn has written for nearly five years as Woodshed columnist for *Bass Player* magazine. The column is based on Glenn's unique instructional methods for aspiring bassists.

At his instructional website, www.glennletsch.com, live, private, online bass lessons are offered to students worldwide. Using technology like IChat AV for Mac and AIM for PC, you can study bass wherever you live.

Email Glenn at glenn@glennletsch.com

HAL LEONARD
BASS METHOD

METHOD BOOKS

by Ed Friedland

BOOK 1
Book 1 teaches: tuning; playing position; musical symbols; notes within the first five frets; common bass lines, patterns and rhythms; rhythms through eighth notes; playing tips and techniques; more than 100 great songs, riffs and examples; and more! The audio includes 44 full-band tracks for demonstration or play-along.
00695067 Book Only $7.99
00695068 Book/Online Audio $12.99

BOOK 2
Book 2 continues where Book 1 left off and teaches: the box shape; moveable boxes; notes in fifth position; major and minor scales; the classic blues line; the shuffle rhythm; tablature; and more!
00695069 Book Only $7.99
00695070 Book/Online Audio $12.99

BOOK 3
With the third book, progressing students will learn more great songs, riffs and examples; sixteenth notes; playing off chord symbols; slap and pop techniques; hammer-ons and pull-offs; playing different styles and grooves; and more.
00695071 Book Only $7.99
00695072 Book/Online Audio $12.99

COMPOSITE
This money-saving edition contains Books 1, 2 and 3.
00695073 Book Only $17.99
00695074 Book/Online Audio $24.99

DVD
Play your favorite songs in no time with this DVD! Covers: tuning, notes in first through third position, rhythms through eighth notes, fingerstyle and pick playing, 4/4 and 3/4 time, and more! Includes 6 full songs and on-screen music notation. 68 minutes.
00695849 DVD $19.95

BASS FOR KIDS
by Chad Johnson

Bass for Kids is a fun, easy course that teaches children to play bass guitar faster than ever before. Popular songs such as "Crazy Train," "Every Breath You Take," "A Hard Day's Night" and "Wild Thing" keep kids motivated, and the clean, simple page layouts ensure their attention remains focused on one concept at a time.
00696449 Book/Online Audio $12.99

REFERENCE BOOKS

BASS SCALE FINDER
by Chad Johnson

Learn to use the entire fretboard with the *Bass Scale Finder*. This book contains over 1,300 scale diagrams for the most important 17 scale types.
00695781 6" x 9" Edition $7.99
00695778 9" x 12" Edition $7.99

BASS ARPEGGIO FINDER
by Chad Johnson

This extensive reference guide lays out over 1,300 arpeggio shapes. 28 different qualities are covered for each key, and each quality is presented in four different shapes.
00695817 6" x 9" Edition $7.99
00695816 9" x 12" Edition $7.99

MUSIC THEORY FOR BASSISTS
by Sean Malone

Acclaimed bassist and composer Sean Malone will explain the written language of music, using easy-to-understand terms and concepts, diagrams, and much more. The audio provides 96 tracks of examples, demonstrations, and play-alongs.
00695756 Book/Online Audio $17.99

STYLE BOOKS

BASS LICKS
by Ed Friedland

This comprehensive supplement to any bass method will help students learn over 200 great bass licks, lines and grooves in many rhythmic styles. *Bass Licks* illustrates how simple melodic patterns can become the springboard for group improvisation or the foundation of a song.
00696035 Book/Online Audio $14.99

BASS LINES
by Matt Scharfglass

500 expertly written bass lines, riffs and fills in a wide variety of musical genres are included in this comprehensive collection to help players expand their bass vocabulary. The examples cover many tempos, keys and feels, and include easy bass lines for beginners on up to advanced riffs for more experienced bassists.
00148194 Book/Online Audio $19.99

BLUES BASS
by Ed Friedland

Learn to play studying the songs of B.B. King, Stevie Ray Vaughan, Muddy Waters, Albert King, the Allman Brothers, T-Bone Walker, and many more. Learn riffs from blues classics including: Born Under a Bad Sign • Hideaway • Hoochie Coochie Man • Killing Floor • Pride and Joy • Sweet Home Chicago • The Thrill Is Gone • and more.
00695870 Book/Online Audio $14.99

COUNTRY BASS
by Glenn Letsch

21 songs, including: Act Naturally • Boot Scootin' Boogie • Crazy • Honky Tonk Man • Love You Out Loud • Luckenbach, Texas (Back to the Basics of Love) • No One Else on Earth • Ring of Fire • Southern Nights • Streets of Bakersfield • Whose Bed Have Your Boots Been Under? • and more.
00695928 Book/Online Audio $17.99

FRETLESS BASS
by Chris Kringel

18 songs, including: Bad Love • Continuum • Even Flow • Everytime You Go Away • Hocus Pocus • I Could Die for You • Jelly Roll • King of Pain • Kiss of Life • Lady in Red • Tears in Heaven • Very Early • What I Am • White Room • more.
00695850..$19.99

FUNK BASS
by Chris Kringel

This is your complete guide to learning the basics of grooving and soloing funk bass. Songs include: Can't Stop • I'll Take You There • Let's Groove • Stay • What Is Hip • and more.
00695792 Book/Online Audio...............................$22.99

R&B BASS
by Glenn Letsch

This book/audio pack uses actual classic R&B, Motown, soul and funk songs to teach you how to groove in the style of James Jamerson, Bootsy Collins, Bob Babbitt, and many others. The 19 songs include: For Once in My Life • Knock on Wood • Mustang Sally • Respect • Soul Man • Stand by Me • and more.
00695823 Book/Online Audio $17.99

ROCK BASS
by Sean Malone

This book/audio pack uses songs from a myriad of rock genres to teach the key elements of rock bass. Includes: Another One Bites the Dust • Beast of Burden • Money • Roxanne • Smells like Teen Spirit • and more.
00695801 Book/Online Audio..............................$21.99

SUPPLEMENTARY SONGBOOKS

These great songbooks correlate with Books 1-3 of the *Hal Leonard Bass Method*, giving students great songs to play while they're still learning! The audio tracks include great accompaniment and demo tracks.

EASY POP BASS LINES
20 great songs that students in Book 1 can master. Includes: Come as You Are • Crossfire • Great Balls of Fire • Imagine • Surfin' U.S.A. • Takin' Care of Business • Wild Thing • and more.
00695810 Book Only..$9.99
00695809 Book/Online Audio................................$15.99

MORE EASY POP BASS LINES
20 great songs for Level 2 students. Includes: Bad, Bad Leroy Brown • Crazy Train • I Heard It Through the Grapevine • My Generation • Pride and Joy • Ramblin' Man • Summer of '69 • and more.
00695819 Book Only..$12.99
00695818 Book/Online Audio................................$16.99

EVEN MORE EASY POP BASS LINES
20 great songs for Level 3 students, including: ABC • Another One Bites the Dust • Brick House • Come Together • Higher Ground • Iron Man • The Joker • Sweet Emotion • Under Pressure • more.
00695821 Book $9.99
00695820 Book/Online Audio................................$16.99

Visit Hal Leonard online at
www.halleonard.com

Prices, contents and availability subject to change without notice.
Some products may not be available outside of U.S.A.

HAL·LEONARD®
BASS
PLAY-ALONG

The Bass Play-Along™ Series will help you play your favorite songs quickly and easily! Just follow the tab, listen to the audio to hear how the bass should sound, and then play-along using the separate backing tracks. The melody and lyrics are also included in the book in case you want to sing, or to simply help you follow along. The audio files are enhanced so you can adjust the recording to any tempo without changing pitch!

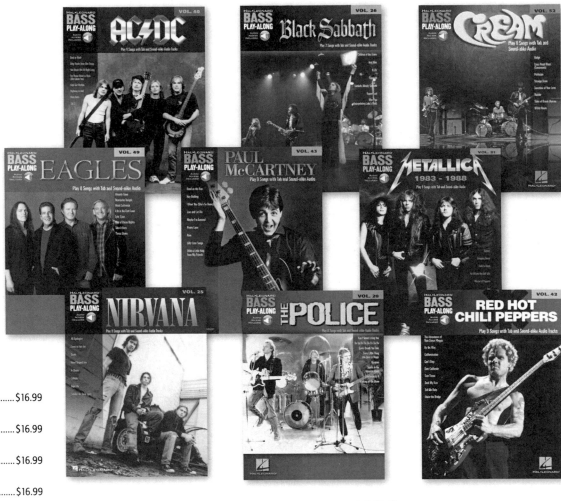

1. Rock
00699674 Book/Online Audio $16.99

2. R&B
00699675 Book/Online Audio $16.99

3. Songs for Beginners
00346426 Book/Online Audio $16.99

4. '90s Rock
00294992 Book/Online Audio $16.99

5. Funk
00699680 Book/Online Audio $16.99

6. Classic Rock
00699678 Book/Online Audio $17.99

8. Punk Rock
00699813 Book/CD Pack $12.95

9. Blues
00699817 Book/Online Audio $16.99

10. Jimi Hendrix – Smash Hits
00699815 Book/Online Audio $17.99

11. Country
00699818 Book/CD Pack $12.95

12. Punk Classics
00699814 Book/CD Pack $12.99

13. The Beatles
00275504 Book/Online Audio $17.99

14. Modern Rock
00699821 Book/CD Pack $14.99

15. Mainstream Rock
00699822 Book/CD Pack $14.99

16. '80s Metal
00699825 Book/CD Pack $16.99

17. Pop Metal
00699826 Book/CD Pack $14.99

18. Blues Rock
00699828 Book/CD Pack $19.99

19. Steely Dan
00700203 Book/Online Audio $17.99

20. The Police
00700270 Book/Online Audio $19.99

21. Metallica: 1983-1988
00234338 Book/Online Audio $19.99

22. Metallica: 1991-2016
00234339 Book/Online Audio $19.99

23. Pink Floyd – Dark Side of The Moon
00700847 Book/Online Audio $16.99

24. Weezer
00700960 Book/CD Pack $17.99

25. Nirvana
00701047 Book/Online Audio $17.99

26. Black Sabbath
00701180 Book/Online Audio $17.99

27. Kiss
00701181 Book/Online Audio $17.99

28. The Who
00701182 Book/Online Audio $19.99

29. Eric Clapton
00701183 Book/Online Audio $17.99

30. Early Rock
00701184 Book/CD Pack $15.99

31. The 1970s
00701185 Book/CD Pack $14.99

32. Cover Band Hits
00211598 Book/Online Audio $16.99

33. Christmas Hits
00701197 Book/CD Pack $12.99

34. Easy Songs
00701480 Book/Online Audio $17.99

35. Bob Marley
00701702 Book/Online Audio $17.99

36. Aerosmith
00701886 Book/CD Pack $14.99

37. Modern Worship
00701920 Book/Online Audio $19.99

38. Avenged Sevenfold
00702386 Book/CD Pack $16.99

39. Queen
00702387 Book/Online Audio $17.99

40. AC/DC
14041594 Book/Online Audio $17.99

41. U2
00702582 Book/Online Audio $19.99

42. Red Hot Chili Peppers
00702991 Book/Online Audio $19.99

43. Paul McCartney
00703079 Book/Online Audio $19.99

44. Megadeth
00703080 Book/CD Pack $16.99

45. Slipknot
00703201 Book/CD Pack $17.99

46. Best Bass Lines Ever
00103359 Book/Online Audio $19.99

47. Dream Theater
00111940 Book/Online Audio $24.99

48. James Brown
00117421 Book/CD Pack $16.99

49. Eagles
00119936 Book/Online Audio $17.99

50. Jaco Pastorius
00128407 Book/Online Audio $17.99

51. Stevie Ray Vaughan
00146154 Book/CD Pack $16.99

52. Cream
00146159 Book/Online Audio $19.99

56. Bob Seger
00275503 Book/Online Audio $16.99

57. Iron Maiden
00278398 Book/Online Audio $17.99

58. Southern Rock
002278436 Book/Online Audio $17.99

Prices, contents, and availability subject to change without notice.

Visit Hal Leonard Online at **www.halleonard.com**